FRENCH
FOR BEGINNERS

Angela Wilkes

Illustrated by John Shackell

Designed by Roger Priddy

Language consultant: Françoise Holmes

CONTENTS

Handlettering by Jack Potter

About this book

This book shows you that learning another language is a lot easier and more fun than you might think. It teaches you the French you will find useful in everyday situations, so you can begin talking to French speakers in their own language.

You can find out how to . . .

talk about yourself,

and your home,

count and tell time,

say what you like,

find your way around

and ask for what you want in shops.

How you learn

Picture strips like this show you what to say in each situation. Read the speech bubbles and see how much you can understand by yourself, then look up any words you do not know. Words and phrases are repeated again and again, to help you remember them.

The book starts with really easy things to say and gets more difficult towards the end.

New words

All the new words you come across are listed on each double page, so you can look them up as you go along. If you forget any words you can look them up in the glossary on pages 46-48. *If you see an asterisk by a word, it means that there is a note about it at the bottom of the page.

Grammar

Boxes like this around words show where new grammar is explained. You will find French easier if you learn some of its grammar, or rules, but don't worry if you don't understand it all right away. You can look up any of the grammar used in the book on pages 42-43.

How to say things

On page 41 you can find out how to pronounce the different letters in French. The best way to find out how to pronounce words, though, is to ask a French teacher or a French friend.

Puzzles

All the way through the book there are puzzles and quizzes to help you practice your French and test yourself on what you have learned.

Practicing your French

Write all the new words you learn in a notebook and try to learn a few every day. Keep going over them and you will soon remember them.

Ask a friend to keep testing you on your French. Even better, ask someone to learn French with you so that you can practice together.

Je voudrais...

Find a French speaker and speak as much French with him or her as you can. Don't be afraid of making mistakes. No one will mind.

Saying "Hello and Goodbye"

The first thing you should know how to say in French is "hello." There are different greetings for different times of the day. Here you can find out what to say when.

In France, it is polite to add **Monsieur**, **Madame** or **Mademoiselle** when you greet people you don't know. You say **Monsieur** to men, **Madame** to women and **Mademoiselle** to girls.

Saying "Hello"

This is how to say "Hello" to your friends.

This is more polite and means "Have a good day."

This is how you say "Good evening" to someone.

Saying "Goodbye"

Salut can mean "Goodbye" as well as "Hello."

These are different ways of saying "See you later."

Saying "Good night"

You only say **Bonne nuit** last thing at night.

4

How are you?

This is how to greet people and ask how they are.

This person is saying that she is fine, thank you . . .

. . . but this one is saying things aren't too good.

Ça va?

This list shows you different ways of saying how you are, from very well to terrible. What do you think each of the people here would say if you asked them how they were?

très bien	very well
bien	well
assez bien	quite well
pas très bien	not very well
très mal	terrible

What is your name?

Here you can find out how to ask people their name and tell them yours, and how to introduce your friends. Read the picture strip and see how much you can understand. Then try doing the puzzles on the opposite page.

New words

je	I
tu	you
il	he
elle	she
ils	they (male)
elles	they (female)
comment	what are
tu t'appelles?	you called?
comment il/elle	what is he
s'appelle?	/she called?
comment ils	what are they
s'appellent?	called?
je m'appelle	I am called
il s'appelle	he is called
elle s'appelle	she is called
ils/elles	they are
s'appellent	called
qui c'est?	who is that?
c'est	that is
mon ami	my friend (male)
mon amie	my friend (female)
et toi?	and you?
oui	yes
non	no

Ils and elles

There are two words for "they" in French: **ils** and **elles**. When you are talking about boys or men, you say **ils** and when you are talking about girls or women, you say **elles**.

If you are talking about boys and girls together, you say **ils**.

Bonjour, comment tu t'appelles?

Max, et toi?

Je m'appelle Monique.

Introducing friends

C'est mon ami. Il s'appelle Pierre.

Qui c'est?

C'est mon amie. Elle s'appelle Marie.

Comment ils s'appellent?

Ils s'appellent Paul et Jean.

6

What are their names?

Can you answer these questions in French?

Comment elle s'appelle, mon amie?

Comment tu t'appelles?

Comment il s'appelle?

Comment ils s'appellent?

Who is who?

Can you answer the questions below the picture?

Salut, ça va?

Ça va bien, merci.

Au revoir, Nicolas.

C'est Anne?

Oui, c'est Anne.

Au revoir.

C'est Jean.

Qui c'est?

Non, je m'appelle Michel.

Tu t'appelles Max?

Comment tu t'appelles?

Pascale, et toi?

Who is talking to Jean?
Who is talking to Pascale?

Who is called Michel?
Who is talking to him?

Who is called Anne?
Who is going home?

Can you remember?

How would you ask people their name?
How would you tell them your name?

You have a friend called Pascale. How would you introduce her to someone?
How would you tell someone your friend is called Daniel?

Finding out what things are called.

Everything in this picture has its name on it. See if you can learn the names for everything; then try the memory test at the bottom of the opposite page. You can find out what **le**, **la** and **l'** mean at the bottom of the page.

la cheminée

le toit

le soleil

l'oiseau

Bonjour!

le nid

l'arbre

la fenêtre

la fleur

la maison

Ça, c'est ma maison.

la porte

le garage

la barrière

le chien

le chat

la voiture

Le and la words

All French nouns are either masculine or feminine. The word you use for "the" shows what gender the noun is. The word for "the" is **le** before masculine (m) nouns, **la** before feminine (f) ones and **l'** before those which start with a vowel. It is best to learn which word to use with each noun. "A" or "an" is **un** before **le** words and **une** before **la** words.

le soleil	sun	**le nid**	nest	**la fenêtre**	window
l'arbre(m)	tree	**l'oiseau(m)**	bird	**la porte**	door
le toit	roof	**le garage**	garage	**la fleur**	flower
le chat	cat	**la maison**	house	**la voiture**	car
le chien	dog	**la cheminée**	chimney	**la barrière**	fence

Asking what things are called

Don't worry if you don't know what something is called in French. To find out what it is, just ask someone **qu'est-ce que c'est?** Look at the list of useful phrases below, then read the picture strip to see how to use them.

qu'est-ce que c'est?	what is that?
c'est . . .	that is . . .
aussi	also
en français	in French
en anglais	in English

Qu'est-ce que c'est ?

C'est une fleur.

C'est aussi une fleur ?

Non, c'est un arbre!

Qu'est-ce que c'est en français ?

C'est une porte.

Et qu'est-ce que c'est ?

C'est un chien.

Qu'est-ce que c'est en anglais ?

A dog !

Can you remember?

Cover up the opposite page and see if you can name all of these things in French. Don't forget to say whether they are **le** or **la** words.

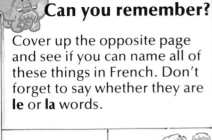

Where do you come from?

Here you can find out how to ask people where they come from. You can also find out how to ask if they speak French.

New words

tu viens d'où?	where do you come from?
je viens de* . .	I come from . .
tu habites où?	where do you live?
j'habite . .	I live in . .
tu parles . . ?	do you speak . . ?
je parle . .	I speak . .
un petit peu	a little
français	French
anglais	English
allemand	German
voici	this is
nous	we
vous	you (plural)

Countries

l'Afrique(f)	Africa
l'Allemagne(f)	Germany
l'Angleterre(f)	England
la France	France
l'Inde(f)	India
l'Écosse(f)	Scotland
l'Autriche(f)	Austria
l'Espagne(f)	Spain
la Hongrie	Hungary

Where do you come from?

Do you speak French?

***De** means "from." Before a word beginning with a vowel, it changes to **d'**: **je viens d'Angleterre** (I come from England).

Who comes from where?

These are the contestants in an international dancing competition. They have come from all over the world. The announcer does not speak any French and does not understand where anyone comes from. Read about the contestants and see if you can tell him what he wants to know. His questions are beneath the picture.

Angus vient d'Ecosse.

Voici Marie et Pierre. Ils viennent de France.

Hari et Indira viennent d'Inde.

Yuri vient de Hongrie. Il habite Budapest.

Franz vient d'Autriche.

Voici Lolita. Elle vient d'Espagne.

Where do they all come from?

Where does Franz come from?
What are the Indian contestants called?
Is Lolita Italian or Spanish?

Is there a Scottish contestant?
Where do Marie and Pierre come from?
Who lives in Budapest? Where is Budapest?

Verbs (action words)	**parler**	to speak	**venir**	to come
French verbs change according to who is doing the action. Verbs ending in **er** follow the same pattern and have the same endings as **parler**. You will have to learn **venir** by itself.*	**je parle**	I speak	**je viens**	I come
	tu parles	you speak	**tu viens**	you come
	il/elle parle	he/she speaks	**il/elle vient**	he/she comes
	nous parlons	we speak	**nous venons**	we come
	vous parlez	you speak	**vous venez**	you come
	ils/elles parlent	they speak	**ils/elles viennent**	they come

Can you remember?

How would you ask people where they come from?

Can you say where you come from?
How do you say that you speak French?
How would you ask others if they can?

*You can find out more about verbs on page 43.

More about you

Here you can find out how to count up to 20, say how old you are and say how many brothers and sisters you have.

To say how old you are in French, you say how many years you have. So if you are ten, you say **J'ai dix ans** (I have ten years).

New words

quel âge as-tu?	how old are you?
j'ai cinq ans	I am five years old
as-tu . . ?	do you have . . ?
j'ai	I have
je n'ai pas de	I have no
des	some, any
le frère	brother
la soeur	sister
presque	almost
ni	nor
mais	but

Plural words

Most French nouns add an "s" in the plural (when you are talking about more than one person or thing), but you don't pronounce it. There are some exceptions which you can see in the glossary. The word for "the" is **les** before all plural nouns.

Numbers*

1	un/une	11	onze
2	deux	12	douze
3	trois	13	treize
4	quatre	14	quatorze
5	cinq	15	quinze
6	six	16	seize
7	sept	17	dix-sept
8	huit	18	dix-huit
9	neuf	19	dix-neuf
10	dix	20	vingt

How old are you?

Do you have any brothers and sisters?

*You will find a complete list of numbers on page 40.

How old are they?

Read what these children are saying. Then see if you can say how old they all are.

Guy a douze ans.

Nous avons quinze ans.

Odile a onze ans.

Michel a presque quatorze ans.

J'ai cinq ans. Il a neuf ans.

Michel   Diane et Sylvie   Guy   Odile   Luc   Colette

How many brothers and sisters?

Below you can read how many brothers and sisters the children have. Can you figure out who has which brothers and sisters?

Diane et Sylvie ont un frère et deux soeurs.

Odile a trois soeurs et deux frères.

Michel a cinq soeurs, mais pas de frères.

Luc a un frère, mais pas de soeurs.

Guy n'a pas de frères ni de soeurs, mais il a un chien.

Useful verbs

avoir	to have
j'ai	I have
tu as	you have
il/elle a	he/she/it has
nous avons	we have
vous avez	you have
ils/elles ont	they have

être*	to be
je suis	I am
tu es	you are
il/elle est	he/she/it is
nous sommes	we are
vous êtes	you are
ils/elles sont	they are

*Etre is used on the next page, so it may help you to learn it now.

Talking about your family

On these two pages you will learn lots of words which will help you to talk about your family. You will also find out how to say "my" and "your" and describe people.

Voici ma famille.

mon chien

mon grand-père

mon père

ma soeur

mon oncle

mon chat

ma grand-mère

ma mère

mon frère

ma tante

Who's who?

C'est ton frère ?

Oui, c'est mon frère ?

Et ça, c'est ta soeur?

Oui, elle s'appelle Nathalie.

Ce sont tes parents ?

Non! Ce sont mes grands-parents!

New words

la famille	family	**la tante**	aunt	**mince**	thin
le grand-père	grandfather	**les grands-parents**	grandparents	**vieux**	old
la grand-mère	grandmother	**les parents**	parents	**jeune**	young
le père	father	**grand/e**	tall	**blond/e.**	blond
la mère	mother	**petit/e**	small	**brun/e**	dark-haired
l'oncle(m)	uncle	**gros/se**	fat	**affectueux/se**	friendly

How to say "my" and "your"

The word you use for "my" or "your" depends on whether you are talking about a **le**, **la** or plural word.*

	my	your
le words	**mon**	**ton**
la words	**ma**	**ta**
plurals	**mes**	**tes**

*You use **mon** or **ton** before words beginning with a vowel. You can find out more about this on pages 42-43.

Describing your family

> Mon père est grand et ma mère est petite.

> Ma mère est grande et mon père est petit.

> Mon oncle est gros et ma tante est mince.

> Mon grand-père est très vieux.* Je suis jeune.

> Ma soeur est blonde. Mon frère est brun.

> Mon chien est affectueux.

Describing words

French adjectives change their endings depending on whether they are describing a **le** or **la** word. In the word list the masculine form is shown, along with the letters you add to make it feminine. The "x" on the end of **affectueux** changes to "se."*

Can you describe each of these people in French, starting **Il est . .** or **Elle est . . ?**

*You can find out more about adjectives on pages 42-43. The feminine of **vieux** is **vieille**.

Your home

Here you can find out how to say what kind of home you live in and where it is. You can also learn the names of all the rooms.

New words

ou	or
la maison	house
l'appartement(m)	apartment
le château	castle
en ville	in town
à la campagne	in the country
au bord de la mer	by the sea
papa	Dad
maman	Mom
pépé	Grandpa
mémé	Grandma
le fantôme	ghost
où êtes-vous?	where are you?
la salle de bains	bathroom
la salle à manger	dining room
la chambre	bedroom
le salon	living room
la cuisine	kitchen
le vestibule	hall
en haut	upstairs

Where do you live?

Tu habites une maison ou un appartement?

J'habite une maison.

J'habite un appartement.

J'habite un château.

Town or country?

J'habite en ville.

J'habite à la campagne.

J'habite au bord de la mer.

Where is everyone?

Papa comes home and wants to know where everyone is. Look at the pictures and see if you can tell him where everyone is, e.g., **Mémé est** **dans le salon**. Then see if you can answer the questions below the little pictures.

Maman   Papa   Pépé

Mémé   Pierre   Isabelle

Simon   le fantôme

Qui est dans la salle à manger?
Qui est dans la cuisine?
Qui est dans la salle de bains?
Qui est dans la chambre?

Où est mémé?
Où est le fantôme?
Où est le chien?
Où est Pierre?
Où est papa? (Look at the word list)

Je suis en haut!

Je suis dans la salle de bains.

Je suis dans la chambre d'Isabelle.

Je suis dans le salon.

Je suis dans la chambre.

Où êtes-vous?

Je suis dans la salle à manger.

Je suis dans la cuisine.

Can you remember?

How do you ask people where they live?
How do you ask if they live in a house or apartment?

Can you remember how to say "in the country"?
Can you remember how to say "in town"?

How would you tell someone you were upstairs?
How would you say you were in the kitchen?

Looking for things

Here you can find out how to ask people what they are looking for and tell them where things are. You can also learn lots of words for things around the house.

New words

chercher	to look for
quelque chose	something
le hamster	hamster
trouver	to find
le	him/it
sur	on
sous	under
derrière	behind
devant	in front of
entre	between
à côté de	next to
le placard	cupboard
l'armoire (f)	closet
le fauteuil	armchair
le rideau	curtain
la plante	plant
le rayon	shelf
la table	table
le tapis	carpet
le canapé	sofa
la télévision	television
le téléphone	telephone
le vase	vase
le voilà!	there it is!

Il or elle?

There isn't a special word for "it" in French. You use **il** or **elle** ("he" or "she") depending on whether the word you are replacing is masculine or feminine. You use **il** to replace masculine words and **elle** to replace feminine ones.

Où est **le** hamster?
Il est sur la table.

Où est **la** tortue?
Elle est sur la table.

The missing hamster

Tu cherches quelque chose?

Je cherche mon hamster. Je ne le trouve pas!

Il n'est pas sur l'armoire.

Il n'est pas sous le canapé.

Il est derrière le rideau?

Non.

Le voilà! Entre les plantes!

In, on or under?

Try to learn these words by heart. **A côté de** changes to **à côte du** when you put it before a **le** word, e.g., **à côté du fauteuil** (next to the armchair).

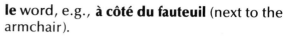

dans   derrière   devant   à côté de   sous   sur

Where are they hiding?

Monsieur Hulot's six pets are hiding somewhere in the room, but he cannot find them. Can you tell him where they are in French, using the words above?

le hamster

le petit chat

le petit chien

la perruche

le serpent

la tortue

le rayon

le vase

le placard

la télévision

le téléphone

le tapis

la table

le fauteuil

le canapé

What do you like to eat?

Here you can find out how to say what you like and don't like.

New words

aimer	to like
tu aimes?	do you like?
j'aime	I like
je n'aime pas*	I don't like
qu'est-ce que . .	what . . ?
adorer	to like a lot
pas du tout	not at all
alors	then
beaucoup	very much
le plus	the most
préférer	to prefer
surtout	best of all
la salade	salad
le poisson	fish
les pommes frites	French fries
le gâteau	cake
la saucisse	sausage
le bifteck	steak
les spaghettis	spaghetti
manger	to eat
la pizza	pizza
le hamburger	hamburger
le riz	rice
le pain	bread
le fromage	cheese
moi aussi	me too

What do you like?

Tu aimes la salade?

Non, je n'aime pas la salade.

Tu aimes le poisson?

Non, pas du tout!

Qu'est-ce que tu aimes, alors?

J'aime les pommes frites.

Et j'adore les gâteaux!

What do you like best?

Qu'est-ce que tu aimes le plus?

J'aime beaucoup les saucisses.

... Mais je préfère le bifteck.

.. Et j'aime surtout les spaghettis!

*You can read more about negatives on pages 42-43.

What are they eating?

Qu'est-ce que tu manges?

Je mange une pizza.

Elle mange des frites.

Il mange du pain et du fromage.

Nous mangeons des hamburgers.

Vous mangez du riz.

Ils mangent des bananes.

Who likes what?

Who likes cheese? Who doesn't like ham? Who prefers grapes to bananas?

Can you say in French which things you like and which you don't like?

Moi aussi, mais je n'aime pas le jambon.

J'aime les bananes.

Je préfère le raisin.

J'aime le fromage.

J'aime surtout la tarte aux fruits.

Jean

Simon

Pépé

Boris

Isabelle

le jambon · le beurre · la quiche

le pain · la salade · les tomates · le fromage

les bananes · le raisin · une tarte aux fruits · le jus d'orange

---

Du, de la, de l' and des

These mean "some" and are often used when there is nothing in English, e.g., **il mange du pain** (he is eating bread). You use **du** before **le** words, **de la** before **la** words, **de l'** before words beginning with a vowel and **des** before plural words.

21

Table talk

Here you can learn all sorts of useful things to say if you are having a meal with French friends or eating out in a French restaurant.

Dinner is ready

New words

à table s'il te plaît	come to the table please
j'ai faim	I'm hungry
moi aussi	me too
sers-toi	help yourself
servez-vous	help yourselves
bon appétit	enjoy your meal
tu peux me passer . .	can you pass me . . .
l'eau(f)	water
le pain	bread
le verre	glass
voulez-vous* . . ?	would you like
encore de . .	some more . .
la viande	meat
oui, s'il te plaît	yes please
non, merci	no, thank you
j'ai assez mangé	I've had enough
c'est bon?	is it good?
c'est délicieux	it's delicious

Please will you pass me . . .

*Vous is a polite way of saying "you." You can find out more about it on page 30.

Would you like some more?

Who is saying what?

These little pictures show you different mealtime situations. Cover up the rest of the page and see if you know what everyone would say in French.

Simon is saying he is hungry.

The chef wants you to enjoy your meal.

Isabelle is saying, "Help yourself."

Pierre wants someone to pass him a glass.

Maman is offering Simon more French fries.

He says, "Yes please," and that he likes French fries.

Then he says, "No thanks." He's had enough.

Marc is saying the food is delicious.

De

De often comes before **le**, **la** or **les** in French, as in **encore de** . . ? (some more . . ?). Before **le** and **les** it changes, as follows:

de + le = du
de + la = de la

de + l' = de l'
de + les = des

Your hobbies

These people are talking about their hobbies.

New words

faire	to do
faire de	
la peinture	to paint
faire la	
cuisine	to cook
le passe-temps	hobby
bricoler	to make things
danser	to dance
lire	to read
regarder	
la télé	to watch TV
tricoter	to knit
nager	to swim
jouer	to play
le sport	sport(s)
le football	soccer
le tennis	tennis
la musique	music
écouter	to listen to
l'instrument (m)	instrument
le violon	violin
le piano	piano
le soir	in the evening

faire (to make or do)

je fais	I do
tu fais	you do
il/elle fait	he/she/it does
nous faisons	we do
vous faites	you do
ils/elles font	they do

jouer à and jouer de

When you talk about playing a sport, you say **jouer à**, then the name of the sport. **A + le** becomes **au**, e.g., **je joue au football** (I play soccer).

To talk about playing an instrument, you say **jouer de**. Remember that **de + le** becomes **du**, e.g., **je joue du piano** (I play the piano).

What do you do in the evenings?

The sporty type

Music lovers

What are they doing?

A

B

C

D

E

Cover up the rest of the page and see if you can say what all these people are doing in French, e.g., **Il joue au football**. What are your hobbies?

Telling time

Here you can find out how to tell time in French. You can look up any numbers you don't know on page 40.

When telling time in French, there is no word for "after"; you just add the minutes to the hour: **Il est neuf heures cinq** (it is five after nine). To say "five to," you say **moins cinq** (minus five): **il est neuf heures moins cinq** (it is five to nine).

New words

quelle heure est-il?	what time is it?
il est une heure	it is one o'clock
il est deux heures	it is two o'clock
moins cinq	five to
et quart	a quarter after
moins le quart	a quarter to
et demie*	half past
midi	noon
minuit	midnight
du matin	in the morning
du soir	in the evening
à	at
se lever	to get up
son	his/her
le petit déjeuner	breakfast
le déjeuner	lunch
le dîner	supper, dinner
il va	he goes
à l'école	to school
au lit	to bed

aller (to go)

je vais	I go
tu vas	you go
il/elle va	he/she goes
nous allons	we go
vous allez	you go (pl)
ils/elles vont	they go

What time is it?

Here is how to ask what time it is.

The time is …

Il est neuf heures cinq.

Il est neuf heures et quart.

Il est neuf heures et demie.

Il est dix heures moins le quart.

Il est dix heures moins cinq.

Il est midi/minuit.

What time of day?

Il est six heures du matin.

Il est six heures du soir.

26   *To say "half past twelve" you say **midi/minuit** et **demi**.

Marc's day

Read what Marc does throughout the day; then see if you can match each clock with the right picture. Go to it! The clocks are ticking.

 a b c d e f g h

1  Marc se lève à sept heures et demie.*	**2**  Il mange son petit déjeuner à huit heures.	**3**  A neuf heures moins le quart, il va à l'école.	**4**  Il mange son déjeuner à midi et demi.
5  A deux heures dix il joue au football.	**6**  A cinq heures et quart il regarde la télé.	**7**  A six heures il mange son dîner.	**8**  Il va au lit à huit heures et demie.

What time is it?

Can you say in French what times these watches and clocks show?

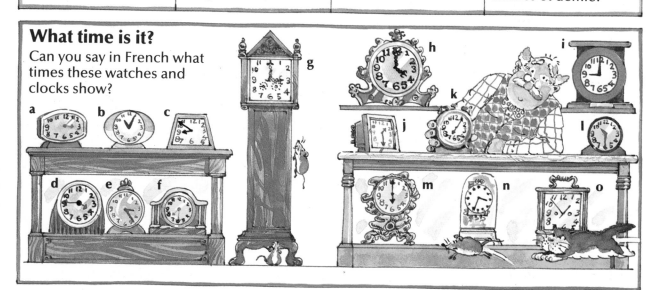

*Some verbs are formed from two parts. You can read about these on pages 42-43.

Arranging things

Here is how to arrange things with your friends.

New words

on va . . ?	shall we go . . ?
quand?	when?
mardi	on Tuesday
le matin	in the morning
l'après-midi (m)	in the afternoon
le soir	in the evening
la piscine	swimming pool
vers	at about
à mardi	until Tuesday
aujourd'hui	today
à demain	until tomorrow
ce soir	this evening
d'accord	O.K.
je ne peux pas	I can't
pas possible	that's no good
dommage	it's a pity!
aller à	to go to
le cinéma	the movies
la partie	party

Days of the week

dimanche	Sunday
lundi	Monday
mardi	Tuesday
mercredi	Wednesday
jeudi	Thursday
vendredi	Friday
samedi	Saturday

Tennis

Swimming

Going to the movies

Going to a party

Your schedule for the week

Here is your schedule, showing what you are doing for a week. Read it and see if you can answer the questions at the bottom of the page in French.

lundi
4 heures. Tennis.

mardi
2 heures. Piano.
5.30 Piscine.

mercredi
3 heures. Tennis.
7.45 Cinéma.

jeudi

Vendredi
8 heures. Danser avec Boris.

Samedi
2 heures. Football.
7 heures. Partie.

dimanche
Tennis l'après-midi.

Qu'est-ce que tu fais vendredi?
Quand joues-tu au tennis?
Tu vas quand au cinéma?
Tu joues du piano jeudi?
Qu'est-ce que tu fais dimanche?
A quelle heure est la partie samedi?

à + le

When **à** comes before **le**, you say **au** instead: **on va au cinéma?** (shall we go to the movies?).*

---

* You can find out more about this on pages 42-43.

Asking where places are

Here and on the next two pages you can find out how to ask your way around.

In French there are two words for "you" – **tu** and **vous**.* You say **tu** to friends, but it is more polite to say **vous** when you talk to adults you don't know well.

New words

pardon	excuse me
je vous en prie	you're welcome
ici	here
là-bas	over there
la poste	post office
sur la place du marché	in the market place
l'hôtel(m)	hotel
puis	then
tournez . .	turn . .
il y a . . ?	is there . . . ?
près d'ici	nearby
la rue	street
juste	just
c'est loin?	is it far?
à cinq minutes	five minutes away
à pied	on foot
le supermarché	supermarket
en face de	across from
à côté de	next to
la banque	bank
la pharmacie	pharmacy

Directions

tout droit

à gauche   **à droite**

Being polite

Pardon, Monsieur...

Merci.

Je vous en prie.

This is how to say "excuse me." It is best to add **Monsieur**, **Madame** or **Mademoiselle**.

When people thank you, it is polite to answer, **"Je vous en prie."**

Where is . . . ?

Pardon, Madame, où est la poste ?

Là-bas, sur la place du marché.

Où est l'Hôtel de la gare, s'il vous plaît ?

Tournez à gauche ici, puis allez tout droit.

 *See pages 42-43.

Is there a . . . nearby?

Is it far?

Other useful places to ask for

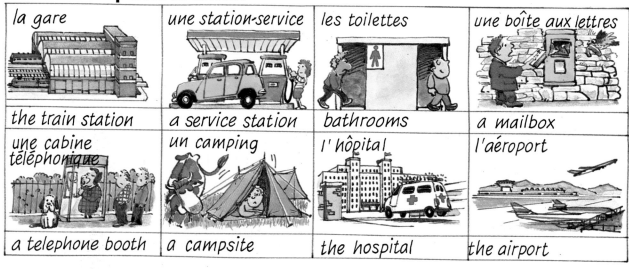

la gare	une station-service	les toilettes	une boîte aux lettres
the train station	a service station	bathrooms	a mailbox
une cabine téléphonique	un camping	l'hôpital	l'aéroport
a telephone booth	a campsite	the hospital	the airport

Finding your way around

Here you can find out how to ask your way around and follow directions. When you have read everything, try the map puzzle on the opposite page.

Pardon, Monsieur, pour aller à la gare, s'il vous plaît ?

Prenez la première à droite, puis la deuxième à gauche.

La gare est à droite.

Pour aller à l'auberge de la jeunesse, s'il vous plaît ?

Allez tout droit jusqu'à la gare...

Puis prenez la troisième rue à droite.

Pour aller au syndicat d'initiative, s'il vous plaît ?

En voiture ? Continuez tout droit...

Puis prenez la première rue à gauche.

x

* **S'il vous plaît** is the polite way to say "please."

New words

pour aller à?	how do I get to?	**jusqu'à**	as far as
prenez . .	take . .	**en voiture**	by car
continuez . .	keep going . . .	**la première rue**	the first street
l'auberge de		**la deuxième rue**	the second street
jeunesse(f)	youth hostel	**la troisième rue**	the third street
le syndicat		**l'Hôtel de Ville**	city hall
d'initiative	tourist office	**l'église(f)**	church

prendre	to take				
		nous prenons	we take	When people are telling you
je prends	I take	**vous prenez**	you take	where to go, they use the
tu prends	you take	**ils prennent**	they take(m)	**vous** part of the verb, e.g.,
il/elle prend	he/she takes	**elles prennent**	they take(f)	**Prenez la première rue** . . .

Finding your way around Beauville

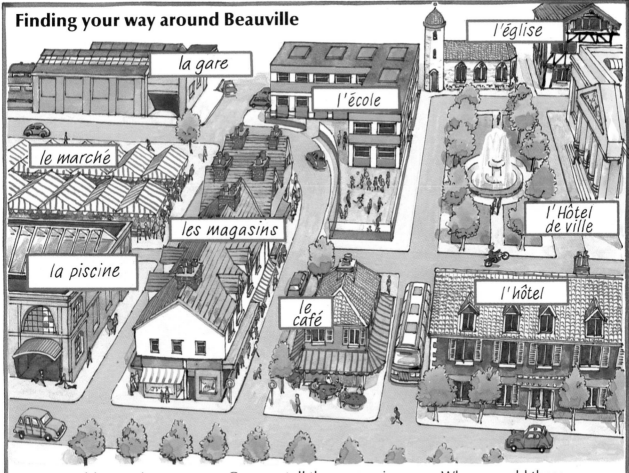

How would you ask someone the way to the market place? How would you ask if there is a café nearby? Ask how far it is.

Can you tell the person in the yellow car how to get to the church?
Can you direct someone from the hotel to the market?

Where would these directions take the yellow car?
Prenez la deuxième rue à gauche et c'est à droite.

Going shopping

Here and on the next two pages you can find out how to say what you want when you go shopping. When you go into a French shop you should say, **"Bonjour, Madame"** (or **Monsieur**). If there are lots of people in there you say, **"Bonjour, Messieurs, Mesdames."**

French money

There are 100 **centimes** in a **franc**. On price tags the word **franc** is shortened to **F**, e.g., **deux francs** is written as **2F**, and **deux francs vingt** as **2F20**. To understand prices you must know the numbers in French. They are listed on page 40.

New words

faire des courses	to go shopping
acheter	to buy
la boulangerie	bakery
l'épicerie(f)	grocery
la boucherie	butcher shop
le lait	milk
l'oeuf(m)	egg
le fruit	piece of fruit
le légume	vegetable
la viande	meat
le petit pain	roll
la pomme	apple
la tomate	tomato
vous désirez?	can I help you?
je voudrais	I would like
oui, bien sûr	with pleasure
c'est tout?	is that all?
et avec ça?	anything else?
ça fait combien?	how much is that?
voilà	there you are
un litre	a liter
un kilo	a kilo
une livre	half a kilo
alors	so, well then

Madame Delon goes shopping

Madame Delon fait des courses.

Elle achète du* pain à la boulangerie.

À la boulangerie

Bonjour, Madame.

Bonjour, Madame.

Je voudrais quatre petits pains.

Oui, bien sûr. C'est tout?

Huit francs, s'il vous plaît!

Oui, merci. Ça fait combien?

Voilà! Merci!

8 F.

*You can read about **du**, **de la** and **de l'** on page 21.

Elle achète du lait et des oeufs à l'épicerie.

Elle achète des fruits et des légumes au marché.

Elle achète de la viande à la boucherie.

À l'épicerie

Au marché

More shopping and going to a café

Here you can find out how to ask how much things cost and how to order things in a café.

New words

coûter	to cost
combien coûte /coûtent?	how much is /are?
la carte postale	postcard
. . . le kilo	. . . a kilo
. . . la pièce	. . . each
la rose	rose
donnez –m'en sept	give me seven
le café	coffee
l'addition(f)	the bill
le raisin	grapes
l'orange(f)	orange
la banane	banana
l'ananas(m)	pineapple
le citron	lemon
la pêche	peach
la limonade	fizzy lemonade
le coca-cola	Coca-Cola
le thé	tea
au lait	with milk
au citron	with lemon
le chocolat	hot chocolate
un verre de	a glass of
une glace	ice cream

Asking how much things cost

Going to a café

36

Buying fruit

Everything on the fruit stand is marked with its name and price.

Look at the picture and see if you can answer the questions below it.

POMMES
4F. 30
le kilo

Vous désirez?

BANANES
4F. 50
le kilo

RAISIN
5F. 20
le kilo

ORANGES
4F. 50
le kilo

ANANAS
4F. 50
la pièce

CITRON
0.60F.
la pièce

PÊCHES
4F. 30
le kilo

How do you tell the vendor you would like four lemons, a kilo of bananas and a pineapple? How much do each of these things cost?

Qu'est-ce qui coûte 4F50 la pièce?
Qu'est-ce qui coûte 4F30 le kilo?
Qu'est-ce qui coûte 5F20 le kilo?
Qu'est-ce qui coûte soixante centimes?

Things to order

Here are some things you might want to order in a café.

Je voudrais...

| une limonade | un coca | un thé au lait | un thé au citron |
| un jus d'orange | un chocolat | un verre de lait | une glace |

The months and seasons

Here you can learn what the seasons and months are called and find out how to say what the date is.

New words

le mois	month
l'année(f)	year
quelle est la date?	what is the date?
aujourd'hui	today
l'anniversaire(m)	birthday

The seasons

le printemps	spring
l'été(m)	summer
l'automne(m)	autumn
l'hiver(m)	winter

The months

janvier	January
février	February
mars	March
avril	April
mai	May
juin	June
juillet	July
août	August
septembre	September
octobre	October
novembre	November
décembre	December

The seasons

le printemps

mars, avril, mai...

l'été

juin, juillet, août...

l'automne

septembre, octobre, novembre...

l'hiver

décembre, janvier, février

First, second, third . . .

For "first" you say **premier** for **le** words and **première** for **la** words. For "second" and so on, you add **ième** to the number, e.g., **deuxième**. If the number ends in "e" you leave the "e" out, e.g., **quatrième** (fourth).*

With dates you say **le premier** for "the first," but for all other dates you just say **le** plus the number.

Janvier est le premier mois de l'année.

Février est le deuxième mois de l'année.

Décembre est le douzième mois de l'année.

Can you say where the rest of the months come in the year?

* **Neuf** (9) becomes **neuvième** (9th).

What is the date?

Aujourd'hui c'est le trois mai.

Quelle est la date aujourd'hui?

Le premier janvier.

Writing the date

Paris, le 3 mai.

Here you can see how a date is written. You put **le**, the number and the month. For "the first" you put **le 1er**.

When is your birthday

C'est quand ton anniversaire?

C'est le dix novembre.

Mon anniversaire est le douze février.

L'anniversaire de Simon est le huit juin.

When are their birthdays?

The dates of the children's birthdays are written below their pictures. Try to say in French when they are, e.g., **L'anniversaire de Nicole est le deux avril**.

Nicole	Bertrand	Hélène	Claire	Claude	Roger

le 2 avril	le 21 juin	le 18 octobre	le 31 août	le 3 mars	le 7 septembre

Colors and numbers

Colors are describing words, so you add "e" when they refer to a **la** word, unless they already end in "e." **Marron** does not change and **blanc** becomes **blanche**.

The colors

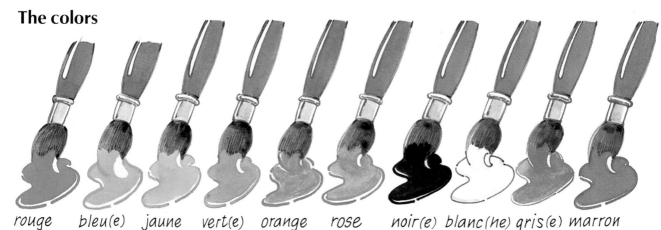

rouge   *bleu(e)*   *jaune*   *vert(e)*   *orange*   *rose*   *noir(e)*   *blanc(he)* *gris(e)* *marron*

What color is it?

Cover the picture above and see if you can say what color everything in the painting is. You should know all the words you need.*

Numbers

You count the 30s, 40s, 50s, 60s and 80s in the same way as 20-29. For 70-79 you add 10-19 to **soixante** (60) and for 90-99 you add 10-19 to **quatre-vingts** (80).

1	un	11	onze	21	vingt et un	40	quarante
2	deux	12	douze	22	vingt-deux	50	cinquante
3	trois	13	treize	23	vingt-trois	60	soixante
4	quatre	14	quatorze	24	vingt-quatre	70	soixante-dix
5	cinq	15	quinze	25	vingt-cinq	71	soixante et onze
6	six	16	seize	26	vingt-six	80	quatre-vingts
7	sept	17	dix-sept	27	vingt-sept	81	quatre-vingt-un
8	huit	18	dix-huit	28	vingt-huit	90	quatre-vingt-dix
9	neuf	19	dix-neuf	29	vingt-neuf	91	quatre-vingt-onze
10	dix	20	vingt	30	trente	100	cent

   *"The sky" is **le ciel**.

Pronunciation guide

In French, many letters are pronounced differently from the way they are said in English. The best way to learn to speak French is to listen carefully to French-speaking people and copy what they say, but here are some general pointers to help you.

Below is a list of letters, with a guide to show you how to pronounce each one. For each French sound, we show an English word (or part of a word) that sounds like it. Read it out loud normally to find out how to pronounce the French sound, then practice saying the examples shown below.

a   Often like the "a" sound in "cart": **arriver, Paris, chat, mari**

e   Like the "a" sound in "above": **le, petit, regarder**

é   Like the "ay" sound in "late": **été, café, thé**

è   Like the "a" sound in "care": **mère, père**

ê   Like the "e" sound in "get": **même, vous êtes**

i   Like the "i" in "machine": **il, dix, police, ville**

o   Like the "o" in "holiday": **fromage, pomme**

u   Round your lips as if you were going to say "oo," then try to say "ee": **du, une, plus, musique**

eau, au   Like the "oa" sound in "toast": **eau, beau, gauche, château**

eu   Like the "u" sound in "fur": **deux, bleu, cheveu**

ou   Like the "oo" sound in "food": **ou, tout, beaucoup**

oi   Like the "wa" sound in "what": **voix, poisson, boîte**

on, an   Like "ong" without the "g" sound at the end: **dans, bonjour, français, Avignon**

un   Like the "u" sound in "sun." You do not pronounce the "n": **un, chacun**

in, ain, im   Like the "an" sound in "rang" without the "g" at the end: **vin, prince, impossible, train**

c   Before "i" or "e," it sounds like the "s" in "sun": **merci, France, certain**

Before other letters, it sounds like the "c" in "cat": **café, coton, crabe**

ç   Like the "s" in "sun": **garçon, français**

ch   Like the "sh" sound in "shirt": **cochon, vache, chanter, Charles**

g   Before "i" or "e," it sounds like the "s" sound in "measure": **gendarme, girafe, âge**

Before other letters, it is like the "g" in "get": **grand, gare, guitare**

gn   Like the "ni" sound in "onion": **campagne, montagne**

j   Like the "s" sound in "measure": **bonjour, jeune**

th   Like the "t" in "top": **thé, théâtre**

qu   Like the "k" sound in "kettle": **question, musique**

h   This letter is not pronounced: **histoire, hôpital, hôtel**

A consonant at the end of a French word is not usually pronounced: **français, petit, les, tout.**

Grammar

Grammar is a set of rules about how to put words together, and it is different for every language. You will find French easier if you learn some of its grammar, but don't worry if you don't understand all of it right away. Just read about it a little at a time. This is a summary of the grammar used in this book.

le, la, l'

In French, every noun is masculine (m) or feminine (f). The word you use for "the" shows whether the noun is masculine or feminine and whether it is singular or plural. The word for "the" is **le** before masculine nouns, **la** before feminine nouns and **l'** before nouns beginning with a vowel.

le livre	the book
la maison	the house
l'arbre (m)	the tree

les

When you are talking about more than one thing the word for "the" is always **les**:

les livres	the books
les maisons	the houses
les arbres	the trees

You add "s" to most nouns to make them plural, but you don't pronounce the "s." Some plurals are formed differently. These are shown in parentheses in the glossary on page 46.

au, aux

If **le** comes after **à**, they join together and become **au**:

Il est au cinéma.   He is at the movies.

à + les becomes **aux**:

la tarte aux fruits   fruit pie

du, des

If **le** comes after **de**, they join together and become **du**:

le prix du pain   the price of the bread

de + les becomes **des**:

le prix des oeufs   the price of the eggs

un, une

The word for "a" or "an" is **un** before masculine nouns and **une** before feminine nouns:

un livre	a book
une maison	a house
un arbre	a tree

some, any

The word for "some" or "any" is **du** before **le** words, **de la** before **la** words, **de l'** before nouns beginning with a vowel and **des** before plurals. The French often say "some" where there is nothing in English:

Il mange du pain.   He is eating bread.

Adjectives

An adjective is a describing word. French adjectives change their endings depending on whether they are describing a masculine or feminine word, and whether the word is singular or plural. In the word lists the masculine singular adjective is shown. You usually add "e" to this to make it feminine, unless it already ends in "e":

il est petit	he is small
elle est petite	she is small

You usually add "s" to an adjective to make it plural:

ils sont petits	they (m) are small
elles sont petites	they (f) are small

My, your

The word for "my" or "your" depends on whether the word that follows it is masculine or feminine, singular or plural:

mon/ton livre	my/your book
ma/ta maison	my/your house
mes/tes frères	my/your brothers

Pronouns

There are two words for "you" in French: **tu** and **vous**. You say **tu** to friends and **vous** when you want to be polite, or when you are talking to someone you don't know well, or when you are talking to more than one person. There are two words for "it": **il** for **le** words and **elle** for **la** words. There are also two words for "they": **ils** for boys, men and **le** words and **elles** for girls, women and **la** words. For masculine and feminine things together, you say **ils**.

I	**je**	he/it (m)	**il**	we	**nous**	they (m)	**ils**	
you	**tu**	she/it (f)	**elle**	you	**vous**	they (f)	**elles**	

Verbs

French verbs (doing words) change according to who is doing the action. Most of them follow regular patterns and have the same endings. The main type of verb used in this book ends in **er**, like **manger** (to eat). You can see the different endings of **er** verbs on the right. There are some verbs in this book that do not follow this pattern, e.g., **avoir**, **être** and **aller**. It is best to learn them as you go along.

manger	to eat
je mange	I eat
tu manges	you eat
il/elle mange	he/she/it eats
nous mangeons	we eat
vous mangez	you eat
ils/elles mangent	they eat

Ne . . . pas

To make a verb negative in French, e.g., to say "I do not...," "he does not...," etc., you put **ne** immediately before the verb and **pas** immediately after it. **Ne** becomes **n'** if the verb begins with a vowel:

Je ne parle pas français.
I do not speak French.

Il n'aime pas le jambon.
He does not like ham.

Reflexive verbs

These are verbs that always have a special pronoun in front of them. Where in English we say "I get up," the French say "I get myself up." The pronoun changes according to who is doing the action, but **me** always goes with **je** and **te** with **tu**, etc., as you can see on the right. **Me** becomes **m'** and **te** becomes **t'** if the verb begins with a vowel: **je m'appelle** (I am called), **tu t'appelles** (you are called).

se lever	to get up
je me lève	I get up
tu te lèves	you get up
il/elle se lève	he/she/it gets up
nous nous levons	we get up
vous vous levez	you get up
ils/elles se lèvent	they get up

Useful words and phrases

Months, seasons and days

The French names for the days of the week, the months of the year and the seasons are all masculine. None of them begin with a capital letter.

The months

January	janvier
February	février
March	mars
April	avril
May	mai
June	juin
July	juillet
August	août
September	septembre
October	octobre
November	novembre
December	décembre

The seasons

spring	le printemps
summer	l'été
autumn/fall	l'automne
winter	l'hiver

The days

Monday	lundi
Tuesday	mardi
Wednesday	mercredi
Thursday	jeudi
Friday	vendredi
Saturday	samedi
Sunday	dimanche

Numbers and telling time

1 **un**	13 **treize**	32 **trente-deux**	80 **quatre-vingts**
2 **deux**	14 **quatorze**	40 **quarante**	81 **quatre-vingt-un**
3 **trois**	15 **quinze**	50 **cinquante**	90 **quatre-vingt-dix**
4 **quatre**	16 **seize**	60 **soixante**	91 **quatre-vingt-onze**
5 **cinq**	17 **dix-sept**	70 **soixante-dix**	92 **quatre-vingt-douze**
6 **six**	18 **dix-huit**	71 **soixante et onze**	100 **cent**
7 **sept**	19 **dix-neuf**	72 **soixante-douze**	101 **cent un**
8 **huit**	20 **vingt**	73 **soixante-treize**	150 **cent cinquante**
9 **neuf**	21 **vingt et un**	74 **soixante-quatorze**	200 **deux cents**
10 **dix**	22 **vingt-deux**	75 **soixante-quinze**	201 **deux cent un**
11 **onze**	30 **trente**	76 **soixante-seize**	500 **cinq cents**
12 **douze**	31 **trente et un**	77 **soixante-dix-sept**	1000 **mille**

Telling time

What time is it?	**Quelle heure est-il?**
It is nine o'clock	**Il est neuf heures**
It is five after nine	**Il est neuf heures cinq**
It is a quarter after nine	**Il est neuf heures et quart**
It is half past nine	**Il est neuf heures et demie**
It is a quarter to ten	**Il est dix heures moins le quart**
It is five to ten	**Il est dix heures moins cinq**
It is noon/midnight	**Il est midi/minuit**

Countries and continents

Africa	l'Afrique (f)	India	l'Inde (f)
Algeria	l'Algérie (f)	Italy	l'Italie (f)
Asia	l'Asie (f)	Japan	le Japon
Australia	l'Australie (f)	Mexico	le Mexique
Austria	l'Autriche (f)	The Netherlands	les Pays Bas (m.pl)
Belgium	la Belgique	New Zealand	la Nouvelle-Zélande
Brazil	le Brésil	North America	l'Amérique du Nord (f)
Canada	le Canada	Poland	la Pologne
China	la Chine	Quebec	le Québec
Denmark	le Danemark	Senegal	le Sénégal
England	l'Angleterre (f)	South America	l'Amérique du Sud
Europe	l'Europe (f)	Soviet Union	l'Union soviétique (f)
France	la France	Spain	l'Espagne (f)
Germany	l'Allemagne (f)	Switzerland	la Suisse
Great Britain	la Grande Bretagne	United States	les Etats-Unis (m.pl)

Useful words and phrases

Yes	Oui
No	Non
Please	S'il vous plaît
I would like . . .	Je voudrais . . .
Thank you	Merci
I'm sorry	Pardon
Excuse me	Excusez-moi
Mr.	Monsieur
Mrs.	Madame
Miss	Mademoiselle
I do not understand	Je ne comprends pas.
I do not speak French.	Je ne parle pas français.
Please speak more slowly.	Plus lentement, s'il vous plaît.

Making friends

Hello	Bonjour
Good evening	Bonsoir
Good night	Bonne nuit
Goodbye	Au revoir
What is your name?	Comment t'appelles-tu?
My name is Roger.	Je m'appelle Roger.
How are you?	Comment vas-tu?
I am fine, thank you.	Je vais bien, merci.

Asking for directions

Where is . . . ?	Où est . . . ?
Where are . . . ?	Où sont . . . ?
How do I get to the train station please?	Pour aller à la gare s'il vous plaît?
You go . . .	Vous allez . . .
Keep going . . .	Vous continuez . . .
You turn . . .	Vous tournez . . .
to the right	à droite
to the left	à gauche
straight ahead	tout droit

Useful places to ask for

airport	l'aéroport
bank	la banque
campsite	le camping
pharmacy	la pharmacie
hospital	l'hôpital
police station	la gendarmerie
post office	le bureau de poste
train station	la gare
tourist office	le syndicat d'initiative
youth hostel	l'auberge de jeunesse

Glossary

Adjectives are shown in their masculine singular form. You just add "e" to make them feminine. The feminine form is only shown when it is different from the usual feminine. Irregular plurals are shown in parentheses next to the letters "pl."

à	at, to
à bientôt	see you soon
à côté de	next to
à droite	on the right
à gauche	on the left
à la campagne	in the country
à peu près	about
à pied	on foot
acheter	to buy
l'addition (f)	check
affectueux, affectueuse	friendly
l'Afrique (f)	Africa
aimer	to like
l'Allemagne (f)	Germany
allemand	German
aller	to go
alors	then
l'ami (m), l'amie (f)	friend
l'ananas (m)	pineapple
anglais	English
l'Angleterre (f)	England
l'année (f)	year
l'anniversaire (m)	birthday
août	August
l'appartement (m)	apartment
l'après-midi (m)	afternoon
l'arbre (m)	tree
l'armoire (f)	closet
assez	enough, quite
l'auberge (f) de jeunesse	youth hostel
au bord de la mer	by the sea
aujourd'hui	today
au revoir	Goodbye
aussi	also, too
l'automne (m)	autumn
l'Autriche (f)	Austria
avec	with
avoir	to have
avoir . . . ans	to be . . . years old
avoir faim	to be hungry
avril	April
la banane	banana
la banque	bank
la barrière	fence
beaucoup	a lot, much, many
le beurre	butter
bien	good, well
bien sûr	of course
le bifteck	steak
blanc, blanche	white
bleu	blue
blond	blond
la boîte aux lettres	mailbox
bon appétit!	Enjoy your meal!
bonjour	Hello, Good Day

bonne nuit	Good Night
bonsoir	Good Evening
la boucherie	butcher shop
la boulangerie	bakery
bricoler	to make things
brun	dark-haired
la cabine téléphonique	telephone booth
le café	café
le camping	campsite
le canapé	sofa
la carte postale	postcard
ça va ?	how are you?
ce, cette	this, that
la chambre	bedroom
le chat	cat
le château (pl.châteaux)	castle
la cheminée	chimney
chercher	to look for
le chien	dog
le chocolat	chocolate
le ciel	sky
le cinéma	the movies
le citron	lemon
le coca-cola	Coca-Cola
combien?	how much?
comment tu t'appelles?	what is your name?
coûter	to cost
la cuisine	kitchen
d'accord	O.K.
dans	in
danser	to dance
décembre	December
le déjeuner	lunch
de l'après-midi	in the afternoon
demain	tomorrow
derrière	behind
deuxième	second
devant	in front of
dimanche	Sunday
le dîner	supper, dinner
dommage!	it's a pity!
d'où?	from where?
du matin	in the morning
du soir	in the evening
l'eau (f)	water
l'école (f)	school
l'Ecosse (f)	Scotland
écouter	to listen to
encore de . . .	more . . .
en face de	across from
en français	in French
en haut	upstairs
entre	between
en ville	in town

en voiture	by car	la	the
l'épicerie (f)	grocery	là-bas	over there
l'Espagne (f)	Spain	le	the
et	and	le lait	milk
l'été (m)	summer	le légume	vegetable
être	to be	la limonade	fizzy lemonade
		le mieux	best
faire	to make, do	lire	to read
faire de la peinture	to paint	le lit	bed
faire des courses	to go shopping	le litre	liter
faire la cuisine	to cook	la livre	half a kilo
la famille	family	le livre	book
le fantôme	ghost	loin	far
le fauteuil	armchair	lundi	Monday
la fenêtre	window		
février	February	madame	Mrs.
la fleur	flower	mademoiselle	Miss
le football	soccer	mai	May
le franc	franc	mais	but
français	French	la maison	house
la France	France	mal	badly
le frère	brother	maman	Mom
le fromage	cheese	manger	to eat
le fruit	fruit	le marché	market
		mardi	Tuesday
le garage	garage	marron	brown
la gare	train station	mars	March
le gâteau (pl. gâteaux)	cake	le matin	morning
la glace	ice cream	mémé	Grandma
grand	tall	merci	thank you
la grand-mère	grandmother	mercredi	Wednesday
le grand-père	grandfather	la mère	mother
les grands-parents	grandparents	midi	midday, noon
gris	gray	mieux	better
gros, grosse	fat	mince	thin
		minuit	midnight
habiter	to live	la minute	minute
le hamburger	hamburger	moi	me
le hamster	hamster	moins	less, minus
l'hiver (m)	winter	le mois	month
la Hongrie	Hungary	mon, ma, mes	my
l'hôtel (m)	hotel	monsieur	Mr., sir
ici	here	nager	to swim
il n'y a pas de quoi	not at all	le nid	nest
il y a	there is, there are	noir	black
l'Inde (f)	India	non	no
		novembre	November
le jambon	ham		
janvier	January	octobre	October
jaune	yellow	l'oeuf (m)	egg
jeudi	Thursday	l'oiseau (m) (pl. oiseaux)	bird
jeune	young	l'oncle (m)	uncle
je vous en prie	you're welcome	orange	orange
jouer	to play	l'orange (f)	orange (fruit)
juillet	July	ou	or
juin	June	où?	where?
le jus d'orange	orange juice	oui	yes
jusqu'à	as far as		
		le pain	bread
le kilo	kilo	papa	Dad

pardon	excuse me
les parents	parents
parler	to speak
pas du tout	not at all
pas possible	that's no good
le passe-temps	hobby
la pêche	peach
pépé	Grandpa
le père	father
la perruche	parakeet
petit	small
le petit chat	kitten
le petit chien	puppy
le petit déjeuner	breakfast
le petit pain	roll
la pharmacie	pharmacy
le piano	piano
la pièce	each (one)
la pizza	pizza
le placard	cupboard
la place du marché	market place
la plante	plant
le poisson	fish
la pomme	apple
les pommes frites	French fries
la porte	door
la poste	post office
premier, première	first
prendre	to take
près d'ici	nearby
presque	almost
le printemps	spring
puis	then
quand?	when?
quel, quelle	what
quelque chose	something
qui?	who?
la quiche	quiche
le raisin	grapes
le rayon	bookshelf
regarder	to watch
le rideau	curtain
le riz	rice
rose	pink
la rose	rose
rouge	red
la rue	street
la salade	salad
la salle à manger	dining room
la salle de bains	bathroom
le salon	living room
Salut!	Hi!, Hello
samedi	Saturday
la saucisse	sausage
se lever	to get up
le serpent	snake
s'il te plaît	please
s'il vous plaît	please (polite)
la soeur	sister
le soleil	sun
le soir	evening
son, sa, ses	his, her, its
sous	under
les spaghettis (m. pl.)	spaghetti
le sport	sport(s)
la station-service	service station
le supermarché	supermarket
sur	on top of
le syndicat d'initiative	tourist office
la table	table
la tante	aunt
le tapis	carpet
la tarte aux fruits	fruit pie
le téléphone	telephone
la télévision	television
le tennis	tennis
le thé	tea
la toilette	bathroom (restroom)
le toit	roof
la tomate	tomato
ton, ta, tes	your (sing.)
la tortue	tortoise
toujours	always
tourner	to turn
tout droit	straight ahead
très	very
tricoter	to knit
troisième	third
trouver	to find
un, une	a, an
le vase	vase
vendre	to sell
vendredi	Friday
venir de	to come from
le verre	glass
vert	green
le vestibule	hall
veux-tu . . . ?	would you like . . . ?
la viande	meat
vieux, vieille	old
le violon	violin
voici!	here is . . . !
voilà!	there is . . . !
la voiture	car

This edition first published in 1999 by Passport Books
A division of NTC/Contemporary Publishing Group, Inc.
4255 West Touhy Avenue, Lincolnwood (Chicago),
Illinois 60646-1975 U.S.A.

Copyright © 1987 Usborne Publishing Ltd.
Printed in Great Britain.

Answers to puzzles

p.7

What are their names?

Il s'appelle Pierre.
Elle s'appelle Marie.
Ils s'appellent Paul et Jean.
Je m'appelle (your name).

Who is who?

Michel is talking to Jean.
Anne is talking to Pascale.
Michel is next to the seal.
Jean is talking to him.
Anne is in the bottom left-hand corner.
The man who is talking to Nicolas is
    going home.

Can you remember?

Comment tu t'appelles?
Je m'appelle . . .
C'est mon amie. Elle s'appelle Pascale.
Mon ami s'appelle Daniel.

p.9

Can you remember?

la/une fleur, le/un chat, l'/un arbre, le/un nid,
l'/un oiseau, le/un toit, le soleil, la/une fenêtre,
la/une voiture, le/un chien

p.11

Who comes from where?

Franz comes from Austria.
They are called Hari and Indira.
Lolita is Spanish.
Yes, Angus comes from Scotland.
Marie and Pierre come from France.
Yuri lives in Budapest.
Budapest is in Hungary.

Can you remember?

Tu viens d'où?
Je viens de . . .
Je parle français.
Tu parles français?

p.13

How old are they?

Michel is 13. Diane and Sylvie are 15. Guy is 12.
Odile is 11. Luc is 9. Colette is 5.

How many brothers and sisters?

A = Diane et Sylvie. B = Luc. C = Michel.
D = Guy. E = Odile.

p.17

Where is everyone?

Simon est dans la cuisine.
Pépé est dans la salle à manger.
Maman est dans la chambre.
Pierre est dans la salle de bains.
Isabelle est en haut.
Le fantôme est dans la chambre d'Isabelle.
Mémé est dans le salon.

Pépé. Simon. Pierre. Maman.

Dans le salon.
Dans la chambre d'Isabelle.
Dans la salle à manger.
Dans la salle de bains.
Dans le vestibule.

Can you remember?

Tu habites où?
Tu habites une maison ou un appartement?
à la campagne
en ville
Je suis en haut.
Je suis dans la cuisine.

p.19

Where are they hiding?

Le hamster est dans le vase.
Le petit chat est derrière la télévision.
Le petit chien est dans le placard.
La perruche est sur le rayon.
Le serpent est derrière le canapé.
La tortue est à côté du téléphone.

p.21

Who likes what?

1. Boris. 2. Jean. 3. Pépé.

p.23

Who is saying what?

"J'ai faim."
"Bon appétit."
"Sers-toi."
"Peux-tu me passer un verre?"
"Veux-tu encore des pommes frites?"
"Oui, merci. J'aime les pommes frites."
"Non, merci. J'ai assez mangé."
"C'est délicieux."

p.25

What are they doing?

A Il fait la cuisine. B Il nage. C Ils dansent.
D Elle joue du violon. E Il fait de la peinture.

p.27

Marc's day

1b, 2e, 3f, 4a, 5h, 6g, 7d, 8c.

What time is it?

A Il est trois heures cinq.
B Il est onze heures cinq.
C Il est neuf heures moins dix.
D Il est quatre heures moins le quart.
E Il est trois heures vingt-cinq.
F Il est sept heures et demie.
G Il est trois heures.
H Il est quatre heures.
I Il est neuf heures.
J Il est une heure et demie.
K Il est sept heures cinq.
L Il est dix heures et demie.
M Il est six heures.
N Il est quatre heures moins vingt-cinq.
O Il est deux heures moins cinq.

p.29

Vendredi soir je vais danser avec Boris.
Je joue au tennis lundi, mercredi et dimanche.

Je vais au cinéma mercredi soir.
Non, je joue du piano mardi.
Dimanche après-midi je joue au tennis.
Elle est à sept heures.

p.33

Pour aller à la place du marché, s'il vous plaît?
Pardon, il y a un café près d'ici?
C'est loin?

Prenez la troisième à gauche, puis allez tout droit.

Prenez la troisième à droite, puis allez tout droit. Le marché est à gauche.

To the school.

p.37

Je voudrais quatre citrons, un kilo de bananes et un ananas.
Quatre citrons coûtent deux francs quarante.
Un kilo de bananes coûte quatre francs cinquante.
Un ananas coûte quatre francs cinquante.

un ananas. les pêches. le raisin. un citron.

p.39

L'anniversaire de Bertrand est le vingt et un juin.
L'anniversaire d'Hélène est le dix-huit octobre.
L'anniversaire de Claire est le trente et un août.
L'anniversaire de Claude est le trois mars.
L'anniversaire de Roger est le sept septembre.

p.40

La rue est grise.
Le soleil est jaune.
Le toit est orange.
Le ciel est bleu.
Les fleurs sont roses.
Le chien est marron.
L'oiseau est noir.
La voiture est rouge.
Les arbres sont verts.
La maison est blanche.